BODY AND GIFT

Pope John Paul II's Theology of the Body
in Simple Language

BOOK ONE
Body and Gift

BOOK TWO
Purity of Heart

BOOK THREE
Heaven and Earth

BOOK FOUR
Love and Life

BODY AND GIFT

Reflections on Creation

Based on a series of talks by
POPE JOHN PAUL II

Adapted into everyday English by
SAM TORODE

With an introduction by
CHRISTOPHER WEST

PHILOKALIA BOOKS

Published by Philokalia Books
P.O. Box 65, South Wayne, Wisconsin 53587

Printed in South Korea

ISBN 0-9725358-1-0

God created Adam and Eve that there
may be great love between them, reflecting
the mystery of Divine unity.

St. Theophilus of Antioch

Contents

> It is an illusion to think we can build a true culture of human life if we do not . . . accept and experience sexuality and love and the whole of life according to their true meaning and their close inter-connection.
>
> — POPE JOHN PAUL II, *The Gospel of Life*

The sexual embrace is the foundation stone of human life itself. The family—and, in turn, culture itself—springs from this embrace. In short, as sex goes, so go marriage and the family. As marriage and the family go, so goes civilization.

Such logic does not bode well for our culture. It's no exaggeration to say that the task of the twentieth century was to rid itself of the Christian sexual ethic. This is why John Paul II devoted the first major teaching project of his pontificate—129 talks delivered between September 1979 and November 1984—to developing a fresh biblical theology of sexual love.

If our culture is to be reclaimed, Christians must first find a way to demonstrate to the modern world that a biblical sexual ethic is not the cramped, prudish list of prohibitions it is assumed to be. Rather, it is a liberating, redeeming path that fulfills the most noble aspirations of the human heart.

This is what John Paul II boldly set out to do in his "theology of the body." The end result is a revolution not only for Catholics, but for *all* Christians, and—if Christians take it up and live it—for the whole world.

Ethics of the Sign

In order to understand the Christian sexual ethic and make it our own, we must follow Christ's words and reflect on God's plan for making us male and female in the first place. According to Jesus, that's the standard. That's the norm. And the "good news" is that Christ came into the world to make God's original plan a reality in our lives.

With this approach—the Gospel approach—John Paul shifts the discussion about sexual morality from legalism ("How far can I go before I break the law?") to liberty ("What is the truth that sets me free?"). The truth that sets us free is salvation in the person of Jesus Christ.

In short, John Paul II's thesis is that the body, in the beauty and mystery of sexual difference and our call to communion, is a sign that makes visible God's invisible mystery. As Trinity, God himself is an eternal communion of love and he has destined us to share in that exchange through Jesus Christ. The male-female communion is meant to be an "echo" in creation of that divine mystery. As St. Paul tells us, the "one flesh" union is "a profound mystery" and it refers to Christ and the Church (Eph. 5:31–32).

As Christians, therefore, we can understand sexual morality through "the ethics of the sign." We should ask ourselves: Is this given behavior an authentic sign of Christ's love, or is it not?

Since sexual union speaks of God's own mystery, it has a "prophetic language." But, as the Pope says, we must be careful to distinguish between true and false prophets. If it is possible to be a "sign" of God's love, it is also possible to be a "countersign." If it is possible to speak the truth with the body, it is also possible to speak a lie.

Who is it that might want us to speak a lie with the body? Could it be the "father of lies"? If God created the body and the communion of the sexes to be the fundamental sign of his own love in the created world, where is the deceiver going to mount his attack? If we want to know what is most sacred in this world, all we need do is look to that which is most violently profaned.

If we are to live the "great mystery" of the body as a sign of Christ's union with the Church, we must be prepared to engage in a lively spiritual battle. And, as St. Paul admonishes, the first thing we must do to prepare for this battle is gird our loins with the truth (Eph 6:14). The theology of the body is a clarion call for all Christians to do just that.

Ecumenical Significance

It's imperative to realize that the theology of the body is not only about marriage and sexual love. Because the communion of the sexes is so intertwined with life itself, the Pope observes that his talks aim at "the rediscovery of the meaning of the whole of existence, the meaning of life." A biblical reflection on the body, the Pope says, plunges us into "the perspective of the whole Gospel, of the whole teaching, in fact, of the whole mission of Christ."

Because the "one flesh" union refers to Christ and the Church, our understanding of sexuality has ramifications for all of theology—for the very way we conceive of Christ and his Church. Thus, it shouldn't surprise us that disputes about the nature of marriage are often at the core of the historical divisions we find in Christianity.

Beyond the wounds and the prejudices, followers of Christ everywhere recognize John Paul II's tireless ecumenical efforts. He has publicly repented on behalf of those Catholics whose sins and betrayals led to division in the first place. He has reached out repeatedly to Protestant and Orthodox leaders, even asking them to help the Catholic Church "re-envision" the papacy so that it could more effectively serve the needs of all Christians.

Yet, one day, Christians may recognize John Paul II's theology of the body as his most important contribution to the unity of the churches. Through this fresh, biblical apologetic for unity in the "domestic church" (the family), John Paul lays the necessary foundation for unity in the Church at large. If disputes in Christ's family have led to multiple divorces, the theology of the body can contribute greatly to bringing Christ's Bride together again in "one body."

Body and Gift

Today, more and more people are hearing about the theology of the body. Still, for the vast majority of Christians, the actual content of the Pope's teaching remains an untapped treasure. In large part, this is because the average person finds the pontiff's dense scholarship almost impenetrable. In this series, Sam Torode provides a tremendous service to all Christians by "translating" the Pope's sublime reflections into "normal" language.

In *Body and Gift*, the first in the series, Sam summarizes and simplifies the 23 talks originally delivered between September 5, 1979 and April 2, 1980. These comprise the first cycle of the theology of the body, "Original Man." (Please see my note on the structure, on page xv.) With Sam's gift for making the Pope's insights accessible, we follow the words of Christ back to our "beginning."

By reflecting on the original experiences of *solitude, unity*, and *nakedness* we discover what it is we have fallen from and, tasting this, we long for the restoration of our "full" humanity. While we can't actually return to the state of innocence, the gift of redemption establishes a connection with our beginning. The heritage of sin carries with it the entire history of discord between the sexes. Yet the roots of the relationship between man and woman go deeper, and, through redemption, Christ enables us to tap in to that deeper heritage.

Moses allowed divorce because he couldn't remove man's "hardness of heart." Christ is able to re-establish "the beginning" as the norm because he is the "Lamb of God who takes away the sins of the world." There is *real power* flowing from Christ's death and resurrection, and it enables men and women to reclaim what was lost.

This is the "good news" John Paul II so powerfully proclaims in his theology of the body. It is my hope that, thanks to this series, even more people encounter the Pope's life-transforming message.

— CHRISTOPHER WEST

Note on Structure

Before venturing into the theology of the body, it's important to understand its basic structure. Through an in-depth reflection on the Scriptures—especially the words of Jesus—John Paul II addresses two universal questions: (1) "What does it mean to be human?" and (2) "How am I supposed to live my life?" These questions frame the project's two main parts. In turn, each of these two parts contains three "cycles" or subdivisions.

Who Are We?

Cycle 1: *Original Man.* This concerns man's experience of sexual embodiment before sin, based on Christ's discussion with the Pharisees about God's plan for marriage "in the beginning" (see Mt. 19:3–9).

Cycle 2: *Historical Man.* This concerns man's experience of sexual embodiment affected by sin yet redeemed in Christ, based on Jesus' words in the Sermon on the Mount regarding adultery committed "in the heart" (see Mt. 5:27–28).

Cycle 3: *Eschatological Man.* This concerns man's experience of sexual embodiment in the resurrection, based on Christ's discussion with the Sadducees regarding the body's resurrected state (see Mt. 22: 23–33).

How Should We Live?

Cycle 4: *Celibacy for the Kingdom*. This is a reflection on Christ's words that some "have renounced marriage because of the kingdom of heaven" (Mt. 19:12).

Cycle 5: *Christian Marriage*. This is primarily a reflection on St. Paul's grand "spousal analogy" in Ephesians 5.

Cycle 6: *Love and Fruitfulness*. This re-examines the Christian sexual ethic in light of the entire preceding analysis, with particular emphasis on the meaning of procreation and the issue of contraception.

In this series, Cycle 1 is covered in *Body and Gift*; Cycle 2 is covered in *Purity of Heart*; Cycles 3 and 4 are covered in *Heaven and Earth*; and Cycles 5 and 6 are covered in *Love and Life*.

BODY AND GIFT

The Beginning

The family is the first community, the basic building block of society and the Church. It has been so from the beginning.

The Lord Jesus uses just this phrase, "from the beginning," in his talk about marriage recorded in the gospels of Matthew and Mark. What exactly did he mean by the "beginning"?

Let's take a close look at the exchange between Jesus and the Pharisees.

> Some Pharisees came to him to test him. They asked, "Is it lawful for a man to divorce his wife for any and every reason?"
>
> "Haven't you read," he replied, "that at the beginning the Creator 'made them male and female,' and said, 'For this reason a man will leave his father and mother and be united to his wife, and the two will become one flesh'? So they are no longer two, but one. Therefore what God has joined together, let man not separate."
>
> "Why then," they asked, "did Moses command that a man give his wife a certificate of divorce and send her away?"
>
> Jesus replied, "Moses permitted you to divorce your wives because your hearts were hard. But it was not this way from the beginning." (Mt. 19:3–8; see also Mk. 10:2–9)

Jesus doesn't answer the Pharisee's question on their level. He didn't approve of their legalistic approach to moral issues, and he wasn't about to get caught up in fruitless arguments. Instead, he refers back to the beginning—to the words of

Genesis, which the Pharisees knew by heart. The Pharisees were looking to test Christ. By going back to God's original blueprint for marriage, he evades their trap and leaves them speechless.

If we want to learn about God's plan for marriage, we have to begin at the beginning. The full text of Genesis 1:27, which Jesus summarizes, says, "So God created man in his own image, in the image of God he created him; male and female he created them." Jesus draws a connection between this verse and Genesis 2:24—"For this reason a man will leave his father and mother and be united to his wife, and the two will become one flesh."

By linking these two verses, and adding, "So they are no longer two, but one. Therefore what God has joined together, let man not separate," Christ casts new light on the "one flesh" union of marriage.

A man and a woman don't become one flesh on their own, Christ says—God unites them. Marriage is not a mere social institution. It is a holy union instituted by God.

Jesus' words, "what God has joined together, let man not separate," are clear. In light of them, we can see that the book of Genesis contains the principle that marriage is a divine union that cannot be dissolved by man.

At this point, it may seem like we've reached a conclusion. But it would be foolish to think we can ever exhaust the rich meaning of Scripture—even of so simple a phrase as "from the beginning." By twice referring his questioners back to the beginning, Jesus asked them to ponder deeply the way God created human beings, precisely as male and female.

Let's put ourselves in the place of Jesus' questioners. But rather than seeking to test Christ, let us meditate on these things, leaning in and looking for wisdom.

In God's Image

The first verse Jesus quoted, Genesis 1:27, comes from the first story of man's creation. This version, told in the first chapter of Genesis, places man within a seven-day cycle of creation.

The other verse Jesus referred to, Genesis 2:24, comes from the second story of man's creation. These two stories are separate but complementary. Starting in Genesis 2, the second account tells the story of Adam and Eve. In detail, it describes man's creation, his original innocence, his happiness, and also his first fall. It extends through the first verse of Genesis 4, where we read about the birth of Adam and Eve's first child. The story of man's creation is then complete.

The first creation story covers the creation of the entire universe, from galaxies and stars down to plants and animals. Leading up to man's creation, there's a steady progression of activity—but then God comes to a pause.

He looks over all the living creatures he's made, and declares them good. Then, God decrees,

> "Let us make man in our image, in our likeness, and let them rule over . . . all the earth"
> So God created man in his own image, in the image of God he created him; male and female he created them. (Gen. 1:26–27)

This first creation story is brimming with theological implications. This is especially true of the way it defines man's relationship to God.

Man is part of the natural world, but, at the same time, he is set apart from it. He isn't like the other animals—he alone is made in God's likeness. That's why he's given stewardship over the earth.

This also explains why man cannot be defined in purely naturalistic or materialistic terms. Yes, man is a physical being. But already, on the first page of the Bible, we learn that man can't be explained as a *merely* physical being—a collection of cells, tissues, and organs. Human beings transcend the categories of chemistry and biology.

Ultimately, man can only be understood in relation to God. This great mystery of creation—that we are created in God's image—is the key reference point for understanding all aspects of humanity, including our sexuality. This is illustrated by the very next verse: "God blessed them and said to them, 'Be fruitful and increase in number; fill the earth and subdue it'" (Gen. 1:28). Thus, to the mystery of man's creation is added the blessing of procreation.

The first chapter of Genesis is the basis for a Christian understanding of man—it tells the truth about who we are as human beings. It is of the utmost importance to all theology, especially the theology of the body.

Original Innocence

The second story of man's creation comes from a different perspective than the first. While the first creation account is objective, the second is subjective—instead of defining man from the outside, it describes life as human beings experience it, from the inside. But the two accounts relate to each other, because all of our subjective experiences correspond to the objective reality that we are created in God's image.

The second creation story is distinguished by its separate account of the creation of the first woman, Eve.

> So the LORD caused the man to fall into a deep sleep; and while he was sleeping, he took one of the man's ribs and closed up the place with flesh. Then the LORD God made a woman from the rib he had taken out of the man, and brought her to the man.
>
> The man said,
> "This is now bone of my bones
> and flesh of my flesh;
> she shall be called 'woman,'
> for she was taken out of man."
>
> For this reason a man will leave his father and mother and be united to his wife, and they will become one flesh.
>
> The man and his wife were both naked, and they felt no shame. (Gen. 2:21–25)

Immediately following this passage, Genesis 3 begins with its account of the Fall of man, linked with that mysterious tree called the "tree of the knowledge of good and evil" (Gen. 2:17).

From then on, Adam and Eve find themselves in an entirely new situation—their world is turned upside down.

In the state of original innocence, Adam and Eve had no knowledge of good and evil. Then, at the prompting of the evil one (in the form of the serpent), they disobeyed God's instruction and ate the fruit of the tree of knowledge. In the second situation, our first parents experienced sin and its consequences.

These two opposite situations correspond to two different aspects of human nature: our created nature and our fallen nature. When Christ referred his questioners back to the beginning, he was directing them to look at man's created nature.

To learn God's intent for marriage, we must look back to that state of original innocence. "Moses permitted you to divorce your wives because your hearts were hard," Jesus says. "But it was not this way from the beginning."

Even though man has lost his innocence and our hearts have grown hard, God's design for marriage hasn't changed.

The Promise of Redemption

When God told Adam not to eat the fruit of the tree of the knowledge of good and evil, he made a covenant with man. But man broke this covenant in his heart. The tree of the knowledge of good and evil stands on the dividing line between two very different situations in Genesis: original innocence and human sinfulness.

But Christ's words to the Pharisees, leading them back to the beginning, show that even though we are now tainted by sin, it is important to remember the state of original innocence. We need to compare our present sinfulness with the way God meant things to be.

When sin entered the world, God responded with a plan for redemption. The first whisper of his promise is found in the "proto-gospel" of Genesis 3:15, where God says,

> "And I will put enmity
> between you [the serpent] and the woman,
> and between your offspring and hers;
> he will crush your head,
> and you will strike his heel."

Starting with Irenaeus, Christian theologians have viewed this text as a foreshadowing of the Gospel—Jesus' victory over Satan. From Genesis 3:15 onward, man lives in the hope of redemption.

Christ's questioners in Matthew 19 were in need of redemption. So are we. We are all participants in the history of human sinfulness, both by the original sin we have inherited and by the personal sins we commit. But we are also called to participate in the history of salvation—the redemption won by Christ's life, death, and resurrection. We may be shut off from the state of original innocence, but we are open to the mystery of redemption.

In his Letter to the Romans, Paul expresses our situation this way: "We ourselves, who have the first fruits of the Spirit, groan inwardly as we wait eagerly for our adoption as sons, the redemption of our bodies" (Rom. 8:23).

We can't lose sight of this hope as we follow the words of Christ, which direct our attention back to the beginning.

Original Solitude

Once again, it seems like we have reached a conclusion. It's tempting to say that now we understand what Christ meant when he referred to the beginning. But let's take another look at the second chapter of Genesis, pondering man's original solitude.

In the second creation story, God says, "It is not good for the man to be alone. I will make a helper suitable for him" (Gen. 2:18). It is significant that this account describes the creation of the first man and the first woman separately.

It is also significant that the first man, "formed from the dust of the ground" (Gen. 2:7), is called a "male" only after the creation of the first woman. "Woman," we read, means "taken out of man" (Gen. 2:23) Masculinity and femininity can only be defined in relation to each other.

So when God, before he creates Eve, says "it is not good for the man to be alone," his statement applies to all mankind. God is speaking of the solitude of "man" (male and female), not just the solitude of the male.

Viewed in this light, "original solitude" has two meanings. The first has to do with human nature: among the living creatures of the earth, human beings are unique and alone. The second has to do with the male/female relationship: without a suitable companion, Adam is alone.

The problem of solitude arises only in the second creation story. The first account doesn't mention a time when man was alone. There, we read only that God created man in his own image, "male and female he created them" (Gen. 1:27). In the second account, the problem of man's solitude is raised before his division into male and female.

The second story tells us that, first and foremost, man was responsible for working the ground (Gen. 2:5). This corresponds to man's vocation to exercise stewardship over the earth (Gen. 1:28). The second story goes on to tell how man was placed in the Garden of Eden, where he lived in happiness amidst "trees that were pleasing to the eye and good for food" (Gen. 2:9). Then, God makes a covenant with man: "You are free to eat from any tree in the garden; but you must not eat from the tree of the knowledge of good and evil, for when you eat of it you will surely die" (Gen. 2:16–17).

This covenant emphasizes man's subjectivity. Man isn't an impersonal *object*, but a *subject* capable of rational thought and communion with God. Man has free will—he can freely choose to keep the covenant, or break it.

Man's dignity as a subject is given more emphasis when God gives him the responsibility of naming the animals: "Now the Lord God had formed out of the ground all the beasts of the field and all the birds of the air. He brought them to the man to see what he would name them, and whatever the man called each living creature, that was its name" (Gen. 2:19).

When Adam names the animals, he discovers the first meaning of his solitude. He realizes that he is in a class by himself, set apart from all the other animals. He is alone. "So the man gave names to all the livestock, the birds of the air and all the beasts of the field. But for Adam no suitable helper was found" (Gen. 2:20).

This passage is leading up to the creation of woman, but

it possesses its own meaning, even apart from Eve's creation. Right from the moment of his creation, man is in search of himself. As we would put it today, he is in search of his own identity. By naming every other living creature, Adam discovers what he is *not*—but he still wonders what he *is*.

Here is the first clue to man's identity: he cannot identify completely with the physical world. The philosopher Aristotle defined man as a "rational animal." He is an animal, yes, but he is distinguished from the other animals by his rationality. Only man possesses language and a moral sense—and these things cannot be explained in terms of the physical world alone.

By exploring the world around him, Adam grew in self-knowledge. By naming the animals, he learned that he was peculiar among all living creatures. And because he was essentially different from the rest of visible world, he was alone.

For the first time, Adam became aware that he was a person.

Person and Body

In just a few verses, the Book of Genesis paints a profound picture of man. He's set above all the other animals; he possesses the power of language; he's a subject in the eyes of God, not an object; and he has free will—the ability to choose his own course of action.

Genesis 1 says that man was created in the image of God. In Genesis 2, he becomes the subject of a covenant with God. A person is meant to be a partner of God. He must discern and choose between right and wrong, life and death. Among all living creatures of the visible world, man alone has been chosen for communion with God. Every human person has a unique, exclusive, unrepeatable relationship with God himself.

Formed from the dust of the ground, man is a physical being—a body among bodies. He participates in the visible world, tilling the ground and transforming his environment into a human habitat, through his body. At the same time, the body is the sign of man's solitude. Man becomes aware that he's a person through the body.

Looking at all the animals, Adam might have concluded that he was one of them. But he didn't. Significantly, he concluded that he was alone.

Later, when Eve is created, Adam understands—as soon as he lays eyes on her—that men and women are fundamentally alike, yet different in complementary ways. Before she even speaks a word, Eve's body reveals all this and more.

The body reveals the person. This phrase tells us all there is to know about the body. Science can examine our flesh in minute detail, down to our cells and even our DNA. But no amount of scientific exploration can replace the truth that our bodies reveal us, giving form to our innermost being and unique personality. Our bodies are sacramental—they make the invisible visible.

Death or Immortality

Through the ages, many philosophers have spoken of man as though he were divided into two distinct parts: soul and body. This isn't the biblical view, though. In Genesis, the fundamental division is not between body and soul, but between dust and breath (life)—between unformed matter and living beings.

Here's how Genesis 2:7 expresses it: "The LORD God formed the man from the dust of the ground and breathed into his nostrils the breath of life, and the man became a living being [or 'living soul']." To create Adam, God did not insert a soul into a body. Instead, Adam entered the world as a unified being, a "living soul" brought to life by the breath of God.

Adam was aware of his unique position from the beginning, since, among animals, he alone was capable of tilling the earth. The human body allows man to carry out distinctly human activities, like gardening. And even though the body is physical, it is almost transparent—it reveals man's identity, giving visible form to his inner life.

Here, with this understanding of his own body, man becomes a partner with God. Making a covenant with Adam, God says, "You are free to eat from any tree in the garden, but you must not eat from the tree of the knowledge of good and evil, for when you eat of it you will surely die" (Gen. 2:16–17).

Up to this point, Adam had only known life; how could he understand the concept of death? The word "die," a completely new one, appears before man has any experience of what it means. But the word is presented as the total opposite of all that Adam has been given. Adam realizes that his life is entirely dependent on God. God breathed life into man, but that breath still belongs to God. When it is taken away, man returns to dust. In this way, the free choice between life and death was set before Adam.

At that moment, the choice between death and immortality became part of what it means to be human. As a living soul called to communion with God, man faced this choice from the beginning.

Original Unity

The words of Genesis 2:18, "It is not good for the man to be alone," are a prelude to the creation of woman. In the narrative of Eve's creation, the theme of original solitude is joined by the theme of original unity.

This is the key to Genesis 2:24, which Jesus quoted in his exchange with the Pharisees: "For this reason a man will leave his father and mother and be united to his wife, and they will become one flesh." Since Christ used this verse in reference to the beginning, we should look closely at the meaning of original unity, which is rooted in the creation of man as male and female.

In the first creation story, there is no mention of man's solitude. Man is "male and female" right from the beginning. But Genesis 2 invites us to think of man before the creation of woman. Only later in the chapter are we invited to think of man in terms of the two sexes.

Original solitude, as we saw, is irrespective of sex. But original unity arises from the union of masculinity and femininity. Male and female are two different incarnations of man. They are two complementary ways of "being a body" created in God's image.

The language of Genesis is mythical, in the sense that it truthfully describes things that are beyond human knowledge. Understood in this way, a "myth" is not a lie, but an ancient and deeper way of knowing. Even with all the discoveries of modern science, we have not surpassed the truths about man found in Genesis. What a marvelous book!

Genesis 2 takes the form of a dialogue between man and his Creator. God says, "It is not good for the man to be alone. I will make a helper suitable for him" (Gen. 2:18). Then, God brings all the animals before the man—but, "For Adam no suitable helper was found" (Gen. 2:20). So, "The LORD God caused the man to fall into a deep sleep; and while he was sleeping, he took one of the man's ribs and closed up the place with flesh. Then the LORD God made a woman from the rib he had taken out of the man, and he brought her to the man" (Gen. 2:21–22).

In preparation for his creative act, God immerses man in sleep—this should give us food for thought. The Hebrew word that the Bible uses for Adam's sleep—*tardemah*—signifies a deep sleep that comes before some extraordinary event. Here, man falls into sleep in order to find a being like himself.

He wakes up "male" and "female." In Genesis 2:23, "She shall be called 'woman' for she was taken out of man," we find the distinction between male and female for the first time. Femininity is found in relation to masculinity, and masculinity is confirmed by femininity. They depend on each other.

Eve is made from the "rib" that God took from Adam's side. This signifies that the male and female bodies share the same physical structure—they are of the same species. It is interesting to note that the ancient Sumerians used the same written sign for "rib" as they used for "life." Adam and Eve share a common source of life—God's breath.

The male and female bodies, though different, share the same humanity. When God brings the woman to Adam, he cries out, "This is now bone of my bones and flesh of my flesh" (Gen. 2:23).

He immediately recognizes her body as a human body, even though she is of a different sex.

In the Bible, the word "bones" expresses a very important aspect of the person. Since the Jews made no distinction between body and soul, the "bones" referred to the very core of one's being.

Adam immediately accepts Eve as a suitable companion. For the first time, man shows joy. He was happy before, but he had no cause for exaltation. Now, in his marriage song, Adam sings, "She is being of my being! A person like me!"

The Communion of Persons

In the Book of Genesis, the creation of man is only complete when he is created as male and female—two beings sharing one human nature, one life, but distinguished by their masculinity and femininity. When men and women were created, God declared them to be "very good" (Gen. 1:31). Adam and Eve were also "very good" in each other's eyes. The woman is for the man, and the man is for the woman.

In one way, Adam was no longer alone after the creation of Eve. But in another way, his solitude as a human being was confirmed in Eve. Adam and Eve were both alone—unique among the animals, unique in their personal relationship to the Creator. Because Adam and Eve shared in this solitude—as all human beings do—they were capable of a deep relationship with each other.

Adam had a personal relationship with God, but he couldn't have a personal relationship with an animal. When God brought Eve to him, he knew right away that here was another body—another person—he could commune with. Together, Adam and Eve became a "communion of persons."

Because we transcend the physical world—being created in the image of God—we are all capable of forming this kind of deep communion with our fellow human beings. It is part of what makes us distinctively human. Living in community, we form bonds and help each other. We live for each other's sake—not just our own.

What enables people to live in communion? Our common human nature, our sharing of the divine image, our free will, and our bodies.

The first creation account tells us that God created man in his own image, *as male and female*. In the second account, the creation of man isn't complete until he exists as male and female—as a communion of persons. From this, we can see that man shares the "image and likeness" not only as an individual human being, but also as a communion of persons.

Adam mirrored the image of God not so much in his solitude, before Eve was created, as after, when he and Eve formed a communion of persons. From the beginning, Adam and Eve reflected God's image through their love for each other. In this way, they mirrored the glory of the *divine* communion of persons—the Holy Trinity. And on this union of man and woman, God bestowed the blessing of fertility.

As Jesus' answer to the Pharisee's question about divorce shows, we cannot understand sexual ethics apart from the truth that the one-flesh union is a sign of God's love. To the extent that they live together in love, man and woman become a picture of the inner life of God. This might be the most amazing thing that we can say about marriage. From the beginning, the male and female bodies were created to form a deep unity.

One Flesh

If we want to know anything about man, first we have to notice that he exists as a dual being, male and female. We have to start with the idea of "communion." Adam and Eve were created to live in unity and harmony. And even in our fallen world, this remains God's design for marriage.

"For this reason," says Genesis 2:24, "a man will leave his father and mother and be united to his wife, and they will become one flesh." When is this union realized? Most clearly, it is expressed when a husband and wife unite sexually, in the marriage act—giving their whole selves to each other and opening themselves to the creation of new life. This intimate union, where a man and a woman cling to each other so closely that they become one flesh, is made possible by our creation as male and female.

Every time a husband and wife come together in this way, they rediscover the mystery of creation. Looking in each other's eyes, they recognize their common humanity, reenacting in a special way that first meeting of man and woman, when Adam declared, "This is now bone of my bones and flesh of my flesh" (Gen. 2:23).

Sex is a powerful bond established by the Creator. But it is far more than just a biological drive. In becoming one flesh, husband and wife are no longer two separate individuals—each takes the other in, expanding the meaning of "self." They are now a communion of persons. The body, through its masculinity and femininity, makes this communion possible.

As Genesis 2 tells us, human beings were created for unity. Right from the beginning, Genesis also indicates, this unity depends on a choice. "For this reason a man will leave his father and mother and be united to his wife" (Gen. 2:24). To become husband and wife, a man and woman must choose to cling to each other. This kind of mutual self-giving can only come about by free choice—it can't be forced.

In all times and places, every time a husband and wife unite so closely as to become one flesh, they discover anew the unifying significance of the body. Each of these unions renews the mystery of creation in all its depth and power. When a husband and wife come together in purity of heart, it is not so much a loss of virginity as a rediscovery of the original, virginal value of man and woman.

Formed in the image of God, and uniting to form a communion of persons, Adam and Eve became the model of marriage for all future couples. That is why Christ appealed to this story in his response to the Pharisees—it was still relevant in Jesus' time, and it is just as relevant today.

Original Nakedness

Genesis 2:25 says, "The man and his wife were both naked, and they felt no shame." At first glance, this detail seems superfluous—far less important, say, than the previous verse about becoming "one flesh." But actually, it introduces us to one of the main elements in the story: the theme of original nakedness. This is, in fact, the key to understanding the biblical vision of man's created nature.

This verse, which says that the first man and woman were "both naked" but "felt no shame," is a description of human consciousness. It takes us inside the minds of Adam and Eve, revealing how they experienced their bodies—both their own and each other's. It describes Adam's experience of femininity as revealed by Eve's naked body, and, at the same time, Eve's experience of masculinity through Adam's body. The author describes this experience in simple, precise words: "they felt no shame."

Several verses later, in the account of man's Fall, we read:

> When the woman saw that the fruit of the tree was good for food and pleasing to the eye, and also desirable for gaining wisdom, she took some and ate it. She also gave some to her husband, who was with her, and he ate it. Then the eyes of both of them were opened, and they realized they were naked; so they sewed fig leaves together and made coverings for themselves. (Gen. 3:1–7)

After breaking their covenant with God, Adam and Eve experience their bodies differently—for the first time, they become conscious of their nakedness and are ashamed. Between Genesis 2:25 and 3:7, there is a fundamental shift.

Before, Adam and Eve were "both naked, and they felt no shame." Now, "they realized they were naked." Does this mean that, before the fall, Adam and Eve didn't really *see* each other's naked bodies? Or has a change taken place on a much deeper level?

It is not simply that Adam and Eve have gone from a state of ignorance to "knowing." Instead, there has been a radical change in the meaning of the original nakedness of man and woman in front of each other. This change emerges from their conscience; it's a fruit of the tree of the knowledge of good and evil.

This change directly involves the way we experience the meaning of bodies. After their eyes are "opened," Adam and Eve first cover their bodies from each other's sight; then they try to hide from God.

> But the Lord God called to the man, "Where are you?"
> He answered, "I heard you in the garden, and I was afraid because I was naked, so I hid." (Gen. 3:8–10)

Shame is a fundamental human experience. Like Adam, we all know what it means to feel shame. In Genesis, this experience marks the border between original innocence and man's sinfulness. To understand what it means to be without shame, and what significance this has for us today, we must look back to the time of original innocence.

Unashamed

Shame is a very complex experience. With shame, a person experiences fear for one's self in the presence of another self (for example, a woman before a man). Shame reveals an instinctive need to be accepted and affirmed by the other. We also experience this need within ourselves—the longing for self-acceptance. Shame is a barrier between persons, but at the same time it seeks to draw them together.

Shame—in particular, sexual modesty—plays an important role in the formation of society by affecting the relationship between the sexes. It expresses the rules for the communion of persons, while also reminding us of our original solitude as individuals before God. But what does the absence of shame mean in the state of original innocence?

We often hear childhood described as a "time of innocence." But it would be misleading to compare Adam and Eve's situation with that of children. The words of Genesis 2:25, "they felt no shame," don't express a lack of development, but a fullness. They indicate that Adam and Eve had a full understanding of the meaning of the body, bound up with their nakedness. When this fullness is lost, shame appears. What, then, is this full understanding of the body and original nakedness?

To answer this question, we have to remember man's original solitude—his aloneness among the other living creatures. This solitude, together with the creation of man as male and female, prepared the way for Adam and Eve's joyful discovery of their shared humanity. At the same time, this discovery was made possible by the body. The naked body was the visible source of this realization, which established their unity.

The words of Genesis 2:25, "The man and his wife were both naked, and they felt no shame," bring us inside the experience of Adam and Eve. This interior perspective is necessary to discover the fullness of interpersonal communication that allowed Adam and Eve to be naked but unashamed.

In our everyday language, the word "communication" usually refers to the news and entertainment media. But in its original and deepest meaning, communication takes place between persons, face to face. We communicate on the basis of our shared humanity.

In light of communication, the body takes on an entirely new meaning, beyond the exterior. It concretely expresses our interior selves. The body enables man and woman, right from the beginning, to communicate with each other as God created them to, in the fullness of a communion of persons.

Original nakedness can only be understood in the context of this communion. The words "they felt no shame" indicate an original depth of understanding between persons. Adam and Eve perfectly accepted each other, affirming each other's masculinity and femininity.

This fullness of understanding, expressed by physical nakedness, parallels our nakedness before God. "Nothing in all creation is hidden from God's sight. Everything is uncovered and laid bare before the eyes of him to whom we must give account" (Heb. 4:13).

Before the Fall, Adam and Eve were truly naked—revealed in all their simplicity and beauty before God and each other.

Creation is a Gift

Adam and Eve were naked before they realized they were naked. In the state of original innocence, they looked upon each other in wonder and gratitude. In this way, they shared the vision of their Creator, who saw all that he had made and declared it "very good" (Gen. 1:31).

"Nakedness" signifies the original goodness of creation in God's eyes. It characterizes the fullness of God's vision, through which we see the high value of man and woman and the purity of sex and the body. At the time of creation, there was no opposition between the physical and the spiritual. There was also no opposition between male and female—the two existed in unity. Adam and Eve looked at each other not just with the exterior gaze of their eyes, but with the eyes of their hearts.

Shame limits our ability to see each other fully. But Genesis 2:25 tells us that Adam and Eve were unashamed. They were not afraid to open up to each other, to become vulnerable. They saw and knew each other intimately, in the peace of their interior gaze. Because they were complementary—Adam's masculinity and Eve's femininity completed each other—they had a special understanding of the meaning of their bodies. They became gifts for each other.

At the beginning, Adam and Eve shared a particular understanding of their bodies as gifts. This is the gift-giving or "nuptial" meaning of the body.

As Christ reminds us, God is the Creator, man is the creature. Genesis uses this word, "create," time and time again to describe God's activity. Why does God create? Why did he call all things from nothingness into being?

Because he is love (1 John 4:8).

We do not find this word—"love"—in the creation story. But the narrative tells us repeatedly, "God saw what he had made, and it was very good." This gives us a glimpse of God's motive in creating, because only love gives birth to goodness and delights in what is good (1 Cor. 13). Creation is a gift. It is a radical form of giving, because God calls forth this gift out of nothingness.

Every creature bears the mark of God's original and fundamental gift. With any gift, there is a relationship established between the giver and the receiver. We see this relationship most clearly in the creation of man—God gave us his image, and this puts us in a unique position with him. Among all creatures, only man is really capable of giving and receiving a gift. Only man can *understand* that creation is a gift, and offer himself to God in return.

Creation is God's gift, bestowed on man. But man is not only the recipient of a gift—he is also a gift himself, with the freedom to give himself to another.

The Body is a Gift

If creation is a gift for man, we have to ask: did Adam live as though the world was a gift? Was he grateful to the Creator?

When God first created Adam, he lived in a state of original happiness. But the Bible does not tell us whether he joyfully embraced the world as an incredible gift. Instead, it focuses on the fact that Adam was alone.

Amidst all the wonders of creation, something was lacking. In Genesis 2:18, for the first time, God notices something that is *not* good: "It is not good for the man to be alone. I will make a helper suitable for him." Adam, too, is keenly aware of this lack. While naming all the animals, he found no suitable helper. No other creature was fit for him; none could unite with him in a relationship of mutual giving.

When God said, "It is not good for the man to be alone," he affirmed that man was created to live in communion. A man reaches his full potential only by living *with* someone—or, even more completely, by living *for* someone.

Human existence is characterized by these two words of Genesis: "alone" and "helper." In a communion of persons, human beings live for each other, as gifts to each other. This is the fulfillment of our original aloneness. When God brings Eve before him, Adam expresses gratitude: "This is now bone of my bones, flesh of my flesh." Adam and Eve were gifts for each other. This mutual gift was expressed by their complementary bodies, male and female.

The body reveals the "living soul" that man became when God breathed life into him. It's a witness to the fact that all of creation is a gift. Because of this, the body is a witness to the Love that brings forth and sustains all life. Our masculinity and femininity—our sex—is the sign of a gift.

By uniting so closely as to become "one flesh," husband and wife open themselves to the blessing of procreation (first spoken of in Genesis 1:28). In Genesis, there is a difference between the sex instinct of animals and the procreative power of human beings. Because man alone is created in the image of God, human sexuality is raised to a higher level—the level of persons.

From the beginning, man's existence as male and female is connected with gift-giving—the nuptial meaning of the body. Human sexuality is fundamentally about mutual self-giving, mirroring the Creator's love.

Free to Love

Freedom lies at the heart of the gift-giving meaning of the body. Before the fall, Adam and Eve were free from the constraints of sin. Naked and unashamed, they weren't oppressed by the urge to misuse each other.

The human body, with its sexuality—male and female—is not only a source of fruitfulness and procreation. It also has the power to express love, allowing the person to become a gift. This self-giving love is unique to human beings—other living creatures reproduce, but they don't love each other in the image of God's love.

Beyond marriage, Christ revealed another vocation for men and women—that of remaining unmarried for the sake of the kingdom of heaven (Mat. 19:12). This only confirms the nuptial meaning of the body. In freedom, we have the power to offer ourselves as a gift—to another person, or even to the kingdom of heaven.

So many people wonder: Who am I? Why am I here on this earth? The answer is found in this self-giving love. We were created by Love, and we're called to love in return. A man can only find his true self by giving himself away. When we live according to the nuptial meaning of our bodies, we fulfil the very meaning of our existence.

In order to make a gift of himself, a man must be free. Adam and Eve were completely free because they were totally innocent. Genesis 2:25 eloquently expresses this freedom: "The man and his wife were both naked, and they felt no shame." For us to achieve freedom, we must learn self-control. The gift-giving, nuptial meaning of the body can only be realized when we're free from sinful passions.

Each human person is willed by God for his own sake. Human life is good in and of itself—it is not a means to an end. Life is sacred, and we cannot put a price on it. Each person is unique and unrepeatable; someone chosen by eternal Love. There has never been, and there will never be, another you.

By giving themselves away, Adam and Eve were able to discover this truth about each other. In their first meeting, Adam found Eve, and Eve found Adam. He accepted her as a unique person, willed by the Creator for her own sake, reflecting the image of God in her femininity. And she accepted him in the same way—as a unique person reflecting the image of God in his masculinity.

The person is affirmed in the accepting of the gift, made possible by the nuptial meaning of the body. This mutual self-giving, first manifested in God's self-giving love, is the basis for the communion of persons. This joyful communion explains why Adam and Eve existed in a state of original happiness. Though this was a short-lived period in human pre-history, comprising only a few verses of Genesis, it is full of implications for the theology of the body. Most particularly, it reveals the nuptial meaning of the body as a gift given in the freedom of love.

The Radiance of Love

The mystery of creation, revealed in the first chapters of Genesis, is that it is a gift from God's boundless love. Only love creates what is good. The sign of love, then, can be found in all created things—especially man. The creation of man as male and female, the nuptial meaning of the body, the original happiness of Adam and Eve—all these things are aglow with the radiance of love.

The opening verses of the Bible speak not only of creation, but of grace. Grace is the communication of God's holiness, the radiance of his Spirit. The first man shone with grace. In the Bible, "first" figuratively means "of God." Adam was not only chronologically the first man, he was called "the son of God" (Luke 3:38).

Happiness is the fruit of love. Man was happy in the beginning because he was created by Love and gave love in return. But even after the Fall, love didn't vanish from the world—because it can never be eradicated. Generations after sin entered the world, Christ came to redeem it—bearing witness to the irreversible love of God first expressed in creation.

As we've seen, man and woman felt no shame in the beginning. Freedom from shame is the result of love. This freedom points us to the mystery of original innocence. Because they were in complete communion with God and each other, Adam and Eve experienced creation at its fullest and deepest dimension. Filled with grace, they walked in God's holiness. This was the source of their innocence. Grace is what enables a man and woman to make a sincere gift to one another.

For Adam and Eve, the body was a witness to innocence. The statement that they were "both naked, but felt no shame," is unique in the Bible. It is never repeated. Elsewhere, nakedness is associated with shame and even disgrace. In the ancient Middle East, clothing was linked to status. Dignified men were well dressed; only slaves and prisoners were naked. In women, nakedness was associated with disrepute.

In this context, we can see just how striking Genesis 2:25 is. Innocence was a gift of grace to Adam and Eve. Because their hearts were pure by the radiation of God's love, they were able to see the true meaning of their nakedness and give themselves completely to each other.

Original innocence speaks of the Creator's gift. It speaks of grace, which enabled man to experience the world as a gift. And it speaks of the self-giving love made possible by the male and female bodies. Above all, original innocence is a matter of the heart and the will. Because of their purity of heart, Adam and Eve were completely faithful to the gift of each other—to the core of their being—with no cause for shame.

A Gift for Each Other

In Genesis, we see the body as a gift, revealed in all its radiant purity—its "nakedness." In the state of original innocence, nakedness wasn't shameful. Nakedness becomes shameful when the woman is an object for the man, or the man an object for the woman. Interior innocence kept Adam and Eve from reducing each other to the level of a mere object. They were united by their shared awareness of the body as a gift.

When does the body cease to be a gift? When we turn it into an object, using it for self-gratification. This denial of the gift marks the end of innocence and the beginning of shame.

In their nakedness and innocence, Adam and Eve gave of themselves and accepted each other. This exchange of the gift involved the whole of their being—their humanity, their masculinity and femininity, their bodies and souls.

At this level, the giving and the receiving are so intertwined that there is almost no distinguishing between them. The two become one—it is difficult to know where giving stops and receiving begins.

In the mystery of creation, the woman is brought to man as a gift. Thanks to original innocence, she is accepted by him as a person good in and of herself, not as an object. Because of the way Adam accepts and welcomes her, Eve discovers herself and the meaning of her femininity. She finds herself because she's been accepted in the way the Creator meant her to be accepted.

From the beginning, the woman was a gift for the man. She was entrusted to his eyes, his sensitivity, his heart. To complete the exchange of the gift, he must give himself to her in return.

This mutual self-giving creates the communion of persons, enriching both the man and the woman. Love begets love.

Innocence and History

Adam and Eve realized they were naked at exactly the point when they ceased to be completely selfless gifts for each other. And, for the first time, they were ashamed.

The Fall radically changed the way man experiences the body. This change involved the interior forces of man—the heart, mind, and will. It also affected man's sensitivity to the gifts of the Holy Spirit. Before the Fall, man was in complete communion with God; but sin separates us from him. We can see what a difference the Fall made by comparing our own experience with that of Adam and Eve as described in Genesis 2.

When Jesus asked, "Haven't you read that at the beginning the Creator 'made them male and female'?" he directed us back to the mystery of creation. We must attempt to follow that direction, fully aware of the gift of original innocence and how original sin separated us from that innocence. We are striving to understand the connection—made by Christ—between original innocence and our historical state after the Fall.

We've tried to discern the original meaning of the body. We've seen how the body becomes a gift when it is given and accepted in freedom and innocence. This truth isn't relevant only to Adam and Eve before the Fall. It is central to God's design for the person and the body, both then and now. Sin has clouded our perception of the design, but it has not changed God's intent.

In the beginning, man and woman were, in a special way, given to each other by the Creator. This gift was not limited to the first couple, Adam and Eve, but extends to the whole human family. Throughout all of history, the fundamental fact of human existence is that God "made them male and female."

After the Fall, man lost his original grace, making it harder to see the nuptial meaning of the body. But the meaning of the gift remains inscribed in the depths of the human heart. Through the veil of shame, man must continually rediscover himself as the guardian of the gift. He must defend the body from being reduced to a mere object.

By looking to the beginning, we can see more clearly who we are as persons, and how we should act. To make of ourselves a gift, and to accept others selflessly—this is the goal to which we should all aspire. For that reason, the nuptial meaning of the body is indispensable for knowing who we are, who we were meant to be, and therefore how we should live in the world.

Body and Sacrament

Man was created as the highest visible expression of God's gift of creation, because he bears the stamp of the gift within himself. Among living creatures, man alone is able to accept the gift. And he has the freedom to give himself in return. Along with this, man brings his particular likeness to God. One aspect of this likeness is his awareness of the nuptial meaning of the body, in the context of original innocence.

At this point in our reflections, we're still at the threshold of man's history. Adam and Eve haven't crossed the boundary of original sin—they're still enraptured by the mystery of creation. The depth of this mystery—its innocence, grace, love, and justice—is hidden in their hearts. "God saw all that he had made, and it was very good" (Gen. 1:31).

The body is a primordial sacrament, a visible sign of God's invisible mystery. This is the mystery of truth and love, of the divine life, in which the human person really participates. The body alone is capable of making visible the invisible. It was created to be a sign of God's love in the visible world.

Through man, created in God's image, the sacramentality of the world is revealed. By means of the physical body, the human person is a visible sign of the love out of which God created all things. Against this vast backdrop, we can understand more fully the sacrament of marriage as it was instituted in the beginning: "For this reason a man will leave his father and mother and be united to his wife, and they will become one flesh" (Gen. 2:24).

Genesis 2:23–25 narrates the first feast of human love, in all its fullness and innocence. Very soon, the shadow of sin and death will darken this holy celebration. But from the beginning, we also have hope. The fruit of love—of which the body is a sign—is not death, but life.

Sex and Knowledge

Man and woman were created for marriage. "For this reason a man will leave his father and mother and be united to his wife, and they will become one flesh" (Gen. 2:24). This introduces a new, creative aspect of human existence—procreation.

Before becoming husband and wife, Adam and Eve emerged from creation as brother and sister sharing the same humanity. Later, Genesis 4:1 (ESV) says: "Now Adam knew Eve his wife, and she conceived and bore Cain, saying, 'I have begotten a man with the help of the Lord.'"

It is interesting that Genesis draws a connection between sex and knowledge: "Adam *knew* his wife." The Hebrew word used here, *jaddah*, doesn't mean "head knowledge" alone; it also refers to concrete experience. Significantly, the experience in which husband and wife unite so closely as to become one flesh is called "knowledge." Throughout the Bible, sex is referred to often in this way. In fact, when the angel Gabriel tells the Virgin Mary that she will give birth to the Savior, she answers, "How can this be, since I do not know a man?"

This term, "knowledge," raises human sexuality above the level of animals to the level of persons. Knowledge refers to the deepest essence of married life. In becoming one flesh, both men and women acquire knowledge through the body. A husband and wife come to "know" the meaning of their bodies. In a unique way, the woman is given to the man to be known, and he is given to her. This experience of the gift mysteriously makes them one, without blurring their individuality.

We all long to be known deeply for who we are. According to Genesis, a man and a woman can know each other in this deep way when they become one flesh.

Three of the Old Testament prophets use this same word, "knowledge," to describe the union of God and his people. In the book of Hosea, God tells his people, "I will betroth you to me in faithfulness, and you shall know the Lord" (2:20 NKJV). This promise is repeated in Isaiah: "Then you will know that I am the Lord." (49:23 NKJV) And again in Ezekiel: "And I will establish my covenant with you. Then you shall know that I am the Lord" (16:62 NKJV).

In the New Testament, Paul takes this further. He tells us that the union between husband and wife is a picture of Christ's love for the Church (Eph. 5:32).

God knows us more than any other person possibly can, and he wants us to know him. Whether we are male or female, married or unmarried, young or old, this is the relationship to which Christ is calling each of us.

Motherhood

The concept of "knowledge" summarizes everything we've talked about thus far. The ability to name something—or someone—is connected with knowledge. Adam named the animals, and he *knew* that he was different from them. This knowledge of his aloneness became the basis for his union with the woman. Because she, too, was created in God's image, Adam was able to know his wife in a way that he could not know an animal. By uniting with her so closely as to become one flesh, he *knew* her. "Adam named his wife Eve," Genesis 3:20 says, "because she would become the mother of all the living."

The mystery of femininity is revealed in motherhood. Men and women are different, not only physically, but even at the deepest psychological levels. And motherhood brings to light the particular power of the female body.

Eve was revealed to Adam as a mother—one in whom new human life is conceived and nurtured. When Eve became a mother, the mystery of Adam's masculinity was also revealed—the lifegiving, fatherly meaning of *his* body.

By revealing the mystery of masculinity and femininity, procreation expands the knowledge shared between man and woman. In sex, a husband and wife know each other, and find themselves affirmed through each other. In procreation, a husband and wife come to know themselves through a *third* person, sprung from them both. This is a revelation. Looking at their child, a husband and wife rediscover themselves, their shared humanity—they see their own living image. When Adam first saw Eve, he declared, "This is now bone of my bones and flesh of my flesh!" And when Eve first saw her child, she exclaimed, "I have begotten a man!"

Those parts of the female body that are connected with motherhood have always been regarded with honor. In the Gospel, a woman says to Jesus, "Blessed is the womb that bore you, and the breasts which nursed you!" (Lk. 11:27 NKJV). These words, spoken in reference to Mary, the second Eve, are a celebration of motherhood and femininity.

When the first Eve became a mother, she praised God: "I have begotten a man with the help of the Lord." Eve's prayer expresses just how significant the blessing of fertility is. The woman's body becomes the place where new human beings are conceived—where the divine image is passed on.

Human beings don't create new life on their own—ultimately, it's God who calls all life into existence. "Before I formed you in the womb I knew you," God told Jeremiah (Jer. 1:5 NKJV).

God not only creates life, he sustains it:

> You are he who took me out of the womb;
> You made me trust while on my mother's breasts.
> I was cast upon you from birth.
> From my mother's womb you have been my God.
> (Psalm 22:9–10 NKJV)

Eve was fully aware of God's work in her life. In bringing forth a child, she knew that she and her husband were working in cooperation with God.

There are many differences between the state of innocence

enjoyed by Adam and Eve in the beginning and the state of sin-fulness they ushered in. But there is also continuity. Even though sin has entered the world, each and every new human being still bears the image of God. This is what gives procreation such immense dignity.

The Cycle of Life

By bringing children into the world, husbands and wives continue the work God began when he created the first man. This is illustrated by Genesis 5, which begins with a brief recap of man's creation, emphasizing that man was created in God's image:

> When God created man, he made him in the likeness of
> God. He created them male and female and blessed them.
> And when they were created, he called them 'man.' When
> Adam had lived 130 years, he had a son in his own likeness,
> in his own image; and he named him Seth. (Gen. 5:1–3)

Since Adam and Eve were the image of God, their children inherited the divine image through them—and so the image is passed on, from generation to generation.

When a man and a woman know each other deeply—so deeply as to become one flesh—they become open to the possibility of procreation. The generation of new life is the fulfillment of the nuptial meaning of their bodies.

Understanding the gift-giving and life-giving meaning of the body, husbands and wives delight in each other and affirm the goodness of life. They become caught up in God's vision at the dawn of creation: "And God saw everything that he had made, and behold, it was very good" (Gen. 1:31).

In their children, they see their own image—and God's—reflected. Every time new life is generated, the world shines with the awe and mystery of creation.

Because of sin, the cycle of life involves not only birth, but suffering and death. After Adam and Eve broke God's covenant with them, God told Eve: "I will greatly increase your pains in childbearing; with pain you will give birth to children" (Gen. 3:16). And to Adam he said, "dust you are and to dust you will return" (Gen. 3:19).

From the moment we come into being, one thing is sure: someday, we'll die. Life and death are locked in a constant struggle. But, in the end, life overcomes death. The cycle of life continues.

In spite of hardship, in spite of suffering and disappointment, in spite of our own sinfulness, and even in spite of death, life is still worth living—and worth giving.

The Total Vision of Man

The Pharisees asked Jesus whether a man should ever divorce his wife. They referred to the law of Moses, which made room for divorce as a human compromise.

"Haven't you read," Christ replied,

> "that at the beginning the Creator 'made them male and female,' and said, 'For this reason a man will leave his father and mother and be united to his wife, and the two will become one flesh'? So they are no longer two, but one. Therefore what God has joined together, let man not separate." (Mt. 19:4–6)

Then, answering the question about Moses, Jesus added:

> "Moses permitted you to divorce your wives because your hearts were hard. But it was not this way from the beginning." (Mt. 19:8)

To find God's intent for marriage, Christ said, we have to go back to the beginning, to the story of man's creation found in Genesis. In these reflections, we've tried to discover the meaning of this "beginning."

Christians believe that the Bible is God's revealed word. And so, to learn the truth about man, the Bible is the first place we turn. There we read that each man and woman is a person created in God's image. What a rich inheritance this truth is!

Christ's answer was directed to the Pharisees, the religious zealots of his day. But his words aren't limited to their original historical setting—they echo throughout all of history. People are still asking tough questions about divorce, and Jesus is still answering them. His words are just as fresh today as the day they were first uttered.

Today, there are many other controversial questions surrounding marriage, sex, and the family.

"What about sex outside of marriage?

"What about homosexuality?"

"What about contraception?"

"What about reproductive technologies?"

They are being asked by singles, couples, and young people; and also by philosophers, scientists, and politicians.

How would Jesus answer these questions? He wouldn't be surprised by them. If his answer to the Pharisees is any indication, he would point us all back to the beginning.

To answer specific questions about marriage, sex, and the family, we first need a "total vision of man." This is why we turn to Genesis. In our scientific age, knowledge has become so specialized that it is easy to lose sight of the whole. The vision of man found in Genesis doesn't require us to renounce science or ignore its findings. Instead, it gives us a solid foundation—a way of understanding what the sciences tell us about man in light of "the image of God."

Genesis is the starting point for the theology of the body. The word "theology" usually refers to the study of God. What can theology have to do with the human body? For Christians, the center of our faith is the Incarnation. When God became flesh—willingly took on a human body—the body entered the halls of theology through the front door.

The Incarnation, together with the redemption won for us by Christ, also raised marriage to the level of a sacrament, a means of receiving God's grace. Christian marriage is far more than a contract or a social arrangement. It is a vocation, a path to holiness and salvation. And a solid, biblical understanding of the body, male and female, is crucial to this vocation.

Because of sin, it is difficult to see the body as a gift, not an object. But for married couples, awareness and acceptance of the gift-giving and life-giving meanings of the body is essential. This is why we need to concentrate on purity of heart in our next series of reflections.

It is so significant that, in answering a question about marriage, Christ directs us back to the time of man's innocence. If, by the beginning, Jesus referred only to our lost innocence, his words would be of little relevance to his questioners and to us. But he is not just pointing back—he is also pointing forward to our redemption.

The promise of redemption bridges the gap between our present sinfulness and our original innocence. A theology of the body is of little use unless we live in the hope of the redemption of the body. In Christ and though Christ, what once was lost can yet be regained.

FURTHER READING

Pope John Paul II, *The Theology of the Body: Human Love in the Divine Plan* (Pauline Books & Media, 1997).

Karol Wojtyla (Pope John Paul II), *Love and Responsibility* (Ignatius Press, 1993).

Mary Shivanandan, *Crossing the Threshold of Love: A New Vision of Marriage* (Catholic University of America Press, 1999).

George Weigel, *The Truth of Catholicism: Ten Controversies Explored* (HarperCollins, 2001), particularly chapter 6, "How Should We Love?"

Christopher West, *Theology of the Body Explained* (Pauline Books & Media, 2003), and *Good News About Sex & Marriage: Answers to Your Honest Questions About Catholic Teaching* (Servant/Charis, 2000).

ACKNOWLEDGMENTS

For valuable guidance, criticism, and encouragement, I would like to thank Christopher West, Fr. John Schroedel, Angela Maupin, George Weigel, Ever Johnson, E. William Sockey, Mary Shivanandan, and my wife, Bethany.

— SAM TORODE

INDEX